JOSEPH HAYDN

SYMPHONY No. 103

E♭ major/Es-Dur/Mi♭ majeur
Hob. I: 103
'Drum Roll'
„Paukenwirbel-Sinfonie"

Edited by/Herausgegeben von
Harry Newstone

Instrumentation:

*Contrapuntal - but mainly violin 1 melody
+ violin 2 & viola harmony*

Wind = double, strengthen + colour
violin: Flutes, oboes, clarinets double melody
Bassoons play bass ← + harmony

Brass Unison as valveless
= pauk, weight

D0238551

Ernst Eulenburg Ltd
London · Mainz · Madrid · New York · Paris · Prague · Tokyo · Toronto · Zürich

CONTENTS/INHALT

Performing material based on this edition is available from the publisher/
Der hier veröffentlichte Notentext ist auch als Aufführungsmaterial beim Verlag erhältlich

© 1996 Ernst Eulenburg & Co GmbH, Mainz
for Europe excluding the British Isles
Ernst Eulenburg Ltd, London
for all other countries

Ernst Eulenburg Ltd
48 Great Marlborough Street
London W1V 2BN

PREFACE/VORWORT

In the autumn of 1790 Prince Nikolaus Joseph Esterházy, Haydn's employer and patron, died and his son, Prince Paul Anton, succeeded him. Almost at once the great (but considerably expensive) musical establishment which had for nearly thirty years nurtured the composer, and is now chiefly remembered for the glory he brought to it, was dismantled. Although still nominally Capellmeister, with a yearly pension, Haydn was at last free to travel wherever he wished, something he had not been able to do before. He returned to Vienna relieved of the daily pressures of court duties, but his respite was not to last long. Johann Peter Salomon, the German-born violinist and London impresario, was visiting Cologne when he heard of the death of Prince Nikolaus and lost no time in getting to Vienna determined to procure Haydn for his forthcoming London season. It was not the first time he had invited Haydn to England; now the composer was free to accept, and he did. A contract was exchanged and the two left Vienna in the middle of December and arrived in Dover on New Year's Day 1791.

Haydn stayed in England for a year and a half and returned for a second visit of similar duration in 1794–5. The stimulus he received from the London musical scene, the reception he was accorded there and the high quality of the musicians placed at his disposal inspired him to some of his finest music. The twelve symphonies he wrote for Salomon (six for each visit) are the summation of his orchestral achievement and the ground upon which the music he composed after his return to Vienna –

Im Herbst 1790 starb Fürst Nikolaus Joseph Esterházy, Haydns Dienstherr und Gönner; Fürst Paul Anton, sein Sohn, folgte ihm nach. Fast unmittelbar hierauf wurde das bedeutende, allerdings ziemlich kostspielige Musikleben am Hofe eingestellt, das Haydn nahezu dreißig Jahre lang ernährt hatte und an das man sich heute hauptsächlich des Glanzes wegen erinnert, den es durch den Komponisten erhalten hatte. Obwohl er auch weiterhin den Kapellmeistertitel führen durfte und eine jährliche Pension erhielt, konnte Haydn im Gegensatz zu früher nun schließlich nach Belieben reisen. Er kehrte nach Wien zurück, entlastet vom täglichen Zwang des Dienstes am Hofe, jedoch sollte diese Ruhepause nicht von langer Dauer sein. Als der deutschstämmige Geiger und Londoner Impresario Johann Peter Salomon während eines Aufenthaltes in Köln vom Tod des Fürsten Nikolaus erfuhr, eilte er unverzüglich nach Wien, entschlossen, Haydn für die kommende Saison nach London zu verpflichten. Dies war nicht das erste Mal, daß er Haydn nach England eingeladen hatte; jetzt jedoch war der Komponist in der Lage zuzusagen, und er tat es auch. Ein Vertrag wurde ausgehandelt, und die beiden verließen Wien Mitte Dezember und erreichten Dover am Neujahrstag 1791.

Haydn blieb anderthalb Jahre lang in England und kehrte 1794/95 zu einem zweiten, etwa gleich langen Aufenthalt zurück. Die Anregungen, die er durch das Londoner Musikleben erhielt, die Aufnahme dort und die hohe Qualität der ihm zur Verfügung stehenden Musiker inspirierten ihn zu mehreren seiner bedeutendsten Werke. So bilden die zwölf Sinfonien für Salomon (sechs für jeden Aufenthalt) die Zusammenfassung seiner ganzen Kunst der Orchesterkomposition und die Grundlage

notably the last six masses, *The Creation* and *The Seasons* – was based.

The most popular of the London symphonies are among the most frequently played of Haydn's works, yet for very many years they were (and often still are) performed from texts that had, during the 19th century, become seriously corrupted from the originals. The first modern attempt to present a uniform set of scores based upon authentic sources came with Ernst Praetorius's edition for Eulenburg in the 1930s. For this he consulted the autograph scores of Nos. 98, 99, 101, 102, 103 and 104 but not those of Nos. 94, 95, 96 and 100 (No. 93 has disappeared and the whereabouts of No. 97 was then unknown). One can only speculate on why Praetorius was not able to examine the autograph of No. 94 which was in the then Preußische Staatsbibliothek in Berlin, where he had seen those of Nos. 98, 99, 101, 102 and 104, or Nos. 95 and 96 which were in the British Museum along with No. 103 of which he had received a photocopy. Clearly, detailed knowledge of the whereabouts of Haydn autographs was still very sketchy in the 1930s and Praetorius probably had no way of knowing what we, with the benefit of a further 50 years of Haydn research, can take for granted. Thus Praetorius's edition, while the best available at the time and certainly an important step in the right direction was, not surprisingly, uneven.

The phase of Haydn research that was to result in no less than a renaissance was now well begun. In 1939 the distinguished Danish scholar Jens Peter Larsen published

für die Werke, die er nach seiner Rückkehr nach Wien schrieb – vor allem die sechs letzten Messen sowie die *Schöpfung* und die *Jahreszeiten*.

Die bekanntesten der Londoner Sinfonien gehören zu den meistgespielten Werken Haydns, jedoch wurden sie viele Jahre lang (vielfach noch bis in die heutige Zeit) aus Notenmaterial aufgeführt, das im 19. Jahrhundert gegenüber dem Originaltext erheblich verfälscht worden war. Den ersten neueren Versuch, aufgrund der authentischen Quellen einen einheitlichen Satz Partituren herauszubringen, stellt die Ausgabe von Ernst Praetorius im Rahmen der Edition Eulenburg in den 1930er Jahren dar. Er zog die Partitur-Autographe von Nr. 98, 99, 101, 102, 103 und 104 heran, nicht aber diejenigen von Nr. 94, 95, 96 und 100 (das Autograph von Nr. 93 ist verschollen, und das von Nr. 97 war damals nicht nachweisbar). Man kann nur Vermutungen darüber anstellen, warum Praetorius nicht in der Lage war, das Autograph von Nr. 94 zu untersuchen, das in der damaligen Preußischen Staatsbibliothek in Berlin lag, wo er auch die Autographe von Nr. 98, 99, 101, 102 und 104 eingesehen hatte; Nr. 95 und 96 waren ihm im British Museum London zugänglich, zusammen mit dem Autograph von Nr. 103, das ihm als Fotokopie vorlag. Auf jeden Fall war die Kenntnis der Aufbewahrungsorte von Haydn-Autographen in den 1930er Jahren noch sehr lückenhaft, und Praetorius konnte damals wohl kaum wissen, was wir heute, nach weiteren 50 Jahren Haydn-Forschung, als erwiesen betrachten können. So war es nicht verwunderlich, daß die Ausgaben von Praetorius in sich unheitlich waren, auch wenn sie zu ihrer Zeit die besten verfügbaren waren und sicherlich einen Schritt in die richtige Richtung unternahmen.

Damit hatte eine Zeit intensiver Haydn-Forschung begonnen, die eine regelrechte Renaissance auslöste. 1939 veröffentlichte der bedeutende dänische Musikwissen-

Die Haydn-Überlieferung and two years later a facsimile print of *Drei Haydn-Kataloge*, revealing for the first time the immensity of the subject. The post-war years saw the formation in London of the Haydn Orchestra and in Boston of the Haydn Society (both 1949). In 1954, the founder of the Haydn Society, H. C. Robbins Landon, in an article *The original versions of Haydn's first 'Salomon' symphonies*,[1] drew our attention to the extent to which the standard performing editions of these works (mostly Breitkopf & Härtel and Peters) were in many cases 'flagrant falsifications of Haydn's own texts'. For a discussion on how these alterations came about the reader is referred to that article as well as to Landon's *The Symphonies of Joseph Haydn*,[2] and his *Haydn – Chronicle and Works*, Vol. 3 *Haydn in England*.[3]

Since the mid-1950s Henle Verlag, Munich, has issued a number of volumes of Haydn symphonies as part of a Complete Edition of his works for the Haydn Institute of Cologne. Universal Edition, Vienna, issued all the symphonies during the 1960s in an edition by H. C. Robbins Landon.

In 1959, the present writer, with material and advice from Professor Landon, revised and conducted all the London symphonies in a series of BBC broadcasts commemorating the 150th anniversary of the composer's death. The aim was to get as close as possible to Haydn's original intentions not only from the scholar's point of view but from the performer's too.

schaftler Jens Peter Larsen sein Buch *Die Haydn-Überlieferung* und zwei Jahre später als Faksimile *Drei Haydn-Kataloge*; damit wies er erstmals auf die nahezu unüberschaubaren Dimensionen dieses Forschungsbereichs hin. In den Nachkriegsjahren folgten die Gründung des Haydn-Orchesters London und in Boston die der Haydn-Gesellschaft (beide 1949). 1954 machte H. C. Robbins Landon, Begründer der Haydn-Gesellschaft, in einem Aufsatz *The original versions of Haydn's first 'Salomon' symphonies*[1] auf das Ausmaß aufmerksam, in dem das verfügbare Aufführungsmaterial dieser Werke (hauptsächlich von Breitkopf & Härtel und Peters) in vielen Fällen durch „offenkundige Verfälschung von Haydns eigenem Notentext" entstellt war. Bezüglich einer eingehenden Darstellung, wie es zu diesen Abweichungen kam, sei hier auf den zitierten Aufsatz sowie auf Landons Arbeiten *The Symphonies of Joseph Haydn*[2] und *Haydn – Chronicle and Works* (Bd. 3 *Haydn in England*)[3] hingewiesen.

Seit Mitte der 1950er Jahre hat der Henle-Verlag München im Rahmen einer Gesamtausgabe der Werke Haydns durch das Haydn-Institut Köln mehrere Bände mit Sinfonien veröffentlicht. Bei der Universal Edition Wien erschienen alle Sinfonien in den 1960er Jahren in einer Ausgabe von H. C. Robbins Landon.

1959 revidierte der Herausgeber der hier vorliegenden Ausgabe anläßlich einer Sendereihe der BBC zum 150. Todestage des Komponisten, in der er selbst alle Londoner Sinfonien Haydns dirigierte, die Partituren, wofür ihm Robbins Landon eigenes Material und seinen Rat zur Verfügung stellte. Das Ziel war, Haydns eigenen Intentionen nicht nur vom wissenschaftlichen Standpunkt aus, sondern auch aus der Sicht des ausübenden Musikers so nahe wie möglich zu kommen.

[1] *The Music Review*, Vol. 15/1, 1954
[2] London, 1955
[3] London, 1976

[1] *The Music Review*, Jg. 15/1, 1954
[2] London 1955
[3] London 1976

The texts were accordingly prepared from a number of manuscript sources of primary authenticity and one early printed edition of unusual interest and importance. These same sources, which are listed below with their credentials, have been re-examined for this new edition together with other more recent discoveries.

Editorial Notes

Location and description of sources

I. Autograph scores and authentic manuscript copies

We retain, for convenience, the generally accepted numerical order established by Eusebius von Mandyczewski for the Breitkopf & Härtel Collected Edition (begun in 1907 but never completed) although, in the case of the first set of London symphonies, this is not thought to be the order in which they were composed or first performed.

No. 93 Autograph:
  Whereabouts unknown, possibly lost. Seen in a Brunswick bookshop in 1870 by the Haydn biographer, Carl Ferdinand Pohl, who noted the date 1791 on it in Haydn's hand.
  Copies:
  1. Copy made in London for Salomon, with corrections in other hands – possibly Haydn's and Salomon's. Acquired by the Royal Philharmonic Society in 1847 from William Ayrton who had inherited all of Salomon's music in 1815. Acquired by the British Library, London, January 1988.[4]
  2. Copy made by Esterházy copyist (Elßler or another with similar handwriting). Esterházy Archives, National Széchényi Library, Budapest.

Der Notentext wurde aufgrund einer Anzahl handschriftlicher Primärquellen und einer besonders interessanten und wichtigen Druckausgabe erarbeitet. Diese unten verzeichneten und beschriebenen Quellen wurden für die Neuausgabe unter Berücksichtigung anderer neuerer Forschungsergebnisse nochmals untersucht.

Revisionsbericht

Quellen-Fundorte und Quellenbeschreibung

I. Partiturautographe und autorisierte Abschriften

Der Einfachheit halber wird die allgemein übliche Zählung nach der Gesamtausgabe von Eusebius von Mandyczewski bei Breitkopf & Härtel (unvollständig, begonnen 1907) beibehalten, obwohl sie vermutlich für die erste Folge der Londoner Sinfonien weder der Reihenfolge der Entstehung noch der Uraufführungen entspricht.

Nr. 93 Autograph:
  Verschollen, möglicherweise verloren. Zuletzt 1870 in einer Braunschweiger Buchhandlung durch den Haydn-Biographen Carl Ferdinand Pohl nachgewiesen, der die Datierung 1791 von Haydns Hand feststellte.
  Abschriften:
  1. Abschrift aus London, angefertigt für Salomon, mit Korrekturen in anderer Handschrift – vermutlich von Haydn und Salomon. 1847 erworben durch die Royal Philharmonic Society London von William Ayrton, der 1815 von Salomon dessen gesamten Bestand an Noten geerbt hatte. Seit Januar 1988 im Besitz der British Library London[4].

---

[4] see Arthur Searle, 'Haydn Manuscripts in the British Library', *Early Music*, 5/1982, also *Haydn Yearbook XIV*

[4] vgl. Arthur Searle, *Haydn Manuscripts in the British Library*, in: *Early Music*, 5/1982, und *Haydn Jahrbuch XIV*

No. 94 Autograph:
Movements I, III and IV in the Staatsbibliothek zu Berlin - Preußischer Kulturbesitz, Musikabteilung, lacking last page of Mov. I and the first two pages of the Minuet. The missing page of Mov. I and the whole of Mov. II (in its original version before Haydn added the 'surprise') in the Library of Congress, Washington, D.C.
Copies:
1. Salomon's London copy; details as No. 93.
2. Esterházy copy; details as No. 93.
Both with later version of Mov. II (i.e., with 'surprise').

No. 95 Autograph:
Royal Philharmonic Society collection, British Library, London. Bound together with autograph of No. 96 and copy of No. 98.
Copies:
None found – see III below.

No. 96 Autograph:
Royal Philharmonic Society collection, British Library, London. Bound together with autograph of No. 95 and copy of No. 98.
Copies:
None found – see III below.

No. 97 Autograph:
Owned by Mrs Eva Alberman, London (formerly Stefan Zweig collection); acquired by the British

---

2. Abschrift eines Kopisten am Hofe Esterházy (Elßler, der Haydns Kopist war, oder jemand mit ähnlicher Handschrift): Esterházy-Archiv der Széchényi-Nationalbibliothek Budapest.

Nr. 94 Autograph:
Satz I, III und IV: Staatsbibliothek zu Berlin - Preußischer Kulturbesitz, Musikabteilung (ohne die letzte Seite von Satz I und die ersten beiden Seiten des Menuetts). Die fehlende Seite von Satz I und der vollständige Satz II (in seiner ursprünglichen Fassung vor der Hinzufügung des „Paukenschlags" durch Haydn) befinden sich in der Library of Congress Washington D.C.
Abschriften:
1. Salomons Londoner Abschrift; wie Nr. 93
2. Abschrift Esterházy: wie Nr. 93 (beide mit der späteren Fassung von Satz II, d.h. mit dem „Paukenschlag")

Nr. 95 Autograph:
Royal Philharmonic Society Sammlung, British Library London (zusammengebunden mit dem Autograph von Nr. 96 und der Abschrift von Nr. 98)
Abschriften:
Nicht nachweisbar (vgl. unten Abschnitt III)

Nr. 96 Autograph:
Royal Philharmonic Society Sammlung, British Library London (zusammengebunden mit dem Autograph von Nr. 95 und der Abschrift von Nr. 98)
Abschriften:
Nicht nachweisbar (vgl. unten Abschnitt III)

Nr. 97 Autograph:
Im Mai 1986 aus dem Besitz von Frau Eva Alberman, London, erworben durch die British Library,

Library, London, May 1986.
Copy:
Salomon's London copy; details
as No. 93.

No. 98 Autograph:
Formerly in the Preußische Staats-
bibliothek, Berlin (from the
Schindler Beethoven collection).
Four pages missing from Mov. IV.
Now in the Jagellonian University
Library, Cracow.
Copy:
Salomon's London copy; details
as No. 93. Bound together with the
autographs of Nos. 95 and 96.

No. 99 Autograph:
Formerly in the Preußische Staats-
bibliothek, Berlin. Now in the
Jagellonian University Library,
Cracow. Photocopy in Hoboken
Photogramm Archiv, Vienna.
Copies:
1. Salomon's London copy; details
as No. 93.
2. Elßler copy, Esterházy Archives,
National Széchényi Library,
Budapest.

No. 100 Autograph:
Esterházy Archives, National Szé-
chényi Library, Budapest, lacking
Mov. II.
Copy:
Salomon's London copy; details
as No. 93.

No. 101 Autograph:
Formerly in the Preußische Staats-
bibliothek, Berlin. Now in the
Jagellonian University Library,
Cracow. Photocopy in Hoboken
Photogramm Archiv, Vienna.
Copies:
1. Salomon's London copy; details
as No. 93.
2. Elßler copy, Esterházy Archives,
National Széchényi Library,
Budapest.

London (vormals Sammlung Stefan
Zweig).
Abschrift:
Salomons Londoner Abschrift; wie
Nr. 93

Nr. 98 Autograph:
Vormals Preußische Staatsbiblio-
thek Berlin (aus der Beethoven-
Sammlung Schindlers). Von Satz
IV fehlen vier Seiten. Heute im
Besitz der Biblioteka Jagiellońska,
Krakau.
Abschrift:
Salomons Londoner Abschrift; wie
Nr. 93 (zusammengebunden mit
den Autographen von Nr. 95 und
96)

Nr. 99 Autograph:
Vormals Preußische Staatsbiblio-
thek Berlin; heute im Besitz der
Biblioteka Jagiellońska, Krakau.
Fotokopien im Photogramm-Archiv
Hoboken, Wien
Abschriften:
1. Salomons Londoner Abschrift;
wie Nr. 93
2. Abschrift Elßler: Esterházy-
Archiv der Széchényi-National-
bibliothek Budapest

Nr. 100 Autograph:
Esterházy-Archiv der Széchényi-
Nationalbibliothek Budapest (ohne
Satz II)
Abschrift:
Salomons Londoner Abschrift; wie
Nr. 93

Nr. 101 Autograph:
Vormals Preußische Staatsbiblio-
thek Berlin; heute im Besitz der
Biblioteka Jagiellońska, Krakau.
Fotokopien im Photogramm-Archiv
Hoboken, Wien
Abschriften:
1. Salomons Londoner Abschrift;
wie Nr. 93
2. Abschrift Elßler: Esterházy-
Archiv der Széchényi-National-
bibliothek Budapest

No. 102 Autograph:
  Staatsbibliothek zu Berlin - Preu-
  ßischer Kulturbesitz, Musikabtei-
  lung, Berlin.
  Copy:
  Salomon's London copy; details
  as No. 93.
No. 103 Autograph:
  British Library, London: three
  pages of Minuet in another hand.
  Copy:
  Salomon's London copy; details
  as No. 93.

No. 104 Autograph:
  Staatsbibliothek zu Berlin - Preußischer Kulturbesitz, Musikabteilung, Berlin.
  Copy:
  Salomon's London copy; details
  as No. 93.

It will be seen that, with the exception of No. 93 and the missing slow movement of No. 100, the autograph scores of the London symphonies have survived very nearly intact. The copies made for Salomon in London are a recent (1982) discovery by Alec Hyatt King, and are of great importance.

II. Manuscript orchestral material by Johann Elßler

Orchestral parts copied from the autograph scores by Haydn's own copyist, many with corrections in the composer's hand, are obviously of great value in the establishment of accurate texts of the London symphonies. The most comprehensive collection of the London symphonies is in the Fürstenberg Archives, Donaueschingen, which has them all but No. 100. Some of these parts are on English paper and were evidently used in the original London performances before being taken back to Vienna by Haydn. The Esterházy Archives in Budapest have Elßler parts of Nos. 95, 96, 97,

Nr. 102 Autograph:
  Staatsbibliothek zu Berlin - Preu-
  ßischer Kulturbesitz, Musikabtei-
  lung
  Abschrift:
  Salomons Londoner Abschrift; wie
  Nr. 93
Nr. 103 Autograph:
  British Library London (drei Sei-
  ten des Menuetts in fremder Hand-
  schrift)
  Abschrift:
  Salomons Londoner Abschrift; wie
  Nr. 93
Nr. 104 Autograph:
  Staatsbibliothek zu Berlin - Preu-
  ßischer Kulturbesitz, Musikabtei-
  lung
  Abschrift:
  Salomons Londoner Abschrift; wie
  Nr. 93

Mit Ausnahme von Nr. 93 und dem fehlenden langsamen Satz von Nr. 100 sind also die autographen Partituren der Londoner Sinfonien nahezu unversehrt erhalten. Die Abschriften, die in London für Salomon angefertigt worden waren, wurden erst kürzlich (1982) von Alec Hyatt King entdeckt; sie sind außerordentlich wichtig.

II. Handschriftliches Orchestermaterial von Johann Elßler

Orchesterstimmen, die nach den autographen Partituren von Haydns eigenem Kopisten geschrieben wurden, viele mit Korrekturen in der Handschrift des Komponisten, sind selbstverständlich von großem Wert bei der Ermittlung eines zuverlässigen Notentextes für die Londoner Sinfonien. Die umfassendste Sammlung ist im Besitz des Fürstenbergischen Archivs in Donaueschingen, wo alle Londoner Sinfonien außer Nr. 100 vorhanden sind. Einige dieser Stimmen sind auf Papier englischer Herkunft geschrieben und offenbar bei den Londoner Aufführungen benutzt worden,

99, 100, 101 and 103 (the latter lacking the Minuet), and the Öttingen-Wallerstein Archives in Harburg have Nos. 93, 96, 97 and 98.

III. London manuscript scores

In 1795 and 1796 respectively, Haydn presented Salomon with the exclusive rights to both sets of London symphonies, a very proper gesture to the man who had commissioned them and had led the orchestra for the first performances of nine of them (the last three symphonies were presented by the newly-formed 'Opera Concert' at the King's Theatre under the direction of Giovanni Battista Viotti). The tangible aspect of this handsome gift was a complete set of scores – the autographs of Nos. 95 and 96 and copies of the rest, as set out in I above. In November 1791, Haydn sent copy scores of Nos. 95 and 96 to his friend in Vienna, Bernhard von Kees. They evidently arrived safely since von Kees entered the opening bars of both works in his catalogue of Haydn symphonies with the words 'NB von London gekommen', but these scores have not been located.

IV. Printed orchestral material by Robert Birchall, London

There can be no doubt that Salomon also had his own personal set of orchestral parts of all 12 symphonies. He had them engraved, after Haydn's return to Vienna (as the terms of the presentation entitled him to do), with at least one publisher (Monzani & Cimador) and he may also have sold them to others. A year or two after Haydn's death (1809) Salomon entered into an agreement with Robert Birchall (who had earlier published Salomon's arrangements for Piano

bevor Haydn sie mit zurück nach Wien nahm. Das Esterházy-Archiv in Budapest besitzt Stimmen von Elßler zu Nr. 95, 96, 97, 99, 100, 101 und 103 (diese ohne Menuett), und das Archiv Öttingen-Wallerstein in Harburg Nr. 93, 96, 97 und 98.

III. Londoner handschriftliche Partituren

1795 bzw. 1796 übertrug Haydn die Exklusivrechte beider Folgen der Londoner Sinfonien an Salomon – eine noble Geste dem Mann gegenüber, der sie in Auftrag gegeben hatte und unter dessen Leitung als Konzertmeister neun von ihnen uraufgeführt worden waren (die letzten drei Sinfonien wurden im King's Theatre vom neu gegründeten „Opera Concert" unter der Leitung von Giovanni Battista Viotti aufgeführt.) Der „materielle Aspekt" dieses noblen Geschenks bestand aus einem vollständigen Satz Partituren – den Autographen von Nr. 95 und 96 und Kopien der restlichen Werke, wie in Abschnitt I ausgeführt. Im November 1791 schickte Haydn Abschriften der Partituren von Nr. 95 und 96 an seinen Wiener Freund Bernhard von Kees. Offenbar sind sie wohlbehalten angekommen, denn von Kees setzte zu den Anfangstakten beider Werke in seinem Verzeichnis der Sinfonien Haydns den Vermerk hinzu: „NB von London gekommen". Die Partituren selbst wurden allerdings bisher nicht aufgefunden.

IV. Gedrucktes Orchestermaterial von Robert Birchall, London

Zweifellos besaß auch Salomon von allen zwölf Sinfonien seinen eigenen Satz Orchesterstimmen. Nach Haydns Rückkehr nach Wien ließ er sie (wozu er nach den Bedingungen der Übereignung berechtigt war) von wenigstens einem Verleger stechen (Monzani & Cimador), und möglicherweise hat er sie außerdem an weitere verkauft. Ein oder zwei Jahre nach Haydns Tod (1809) schloß Salomon eine Vereinbarung mit Robert Birchall (der schon zuvor Salo-

Trio and for Flute and String Quartet with optional Piano of the London symphonies) for a new issue of the orchestral parts. If Landon is right in supposing that Salomon provided Birchall with his own performing material for this print – possibly the very material he had used under Haydn's direction – it would explain not only the high intelligence and practical nature of the editings, but, more important, the often close relationship between Birchall and the autographs, and the even closer relationship between Birchall and the copy scores that Haydn presented to Salomon.

The Birchall print thus has a high place among the sources upon which this edition is based. With so strong a link – Salomon – between it and Haydn and its readiness as a performing edition, it has a combination of virtues that will be of interest to both scholars and performers. Where the Birchall differs from our other sources (generally because of changes that Haydn made after his return to Vienna that would have been unknown to Salomon) such variants, as well as others of interest, are shown in the Textual Notes below.

Editorial method

Redundant cautionary or parallel accidentals have in some cases been omitted. Haydn's habit of reminding players constantly of such accidentals in continuously modulating passages, even if it means repeating them in the same bar, makes it difficult to follow this aim with complete consistency, and in such cases we have omitted only those which, in modern practice, might confuse rather than clarify.

mons Bearbeitungen der Londoner Sinfonien für Klaviertrio sowie für Flöte und Streichquartett und Klavier ad libitum veröffentlicht hatte) über eine Neuausgabe der Orchesterstimmen. Falls Landon mit seiner Annahme recht hat, daß Salomon für diesen Druck Birchall sein eigenes Orchestermaterial zur Verfügung stellte – möglicherweise dasselbe Material, das er bereits unter Haydns Leitung benutzt hatte –, würde dies nicht nur den hohen Standard und den praktischen Charakter der Ausgaben erklären, sondern darüber hinaus auch die oft enge Beziehung zwischen den Stimmen von Birchall und den Autographen und – mit sogar noch größerer Übereinstimmung – zwischen dem Birchall-Druck und den Partitur-Abschriften, die Haydn Salomon geschenkt hatte.

Der Birchall-Druck besitzt also unter den Quellen, auf denen die vorliegende Edition basiert, einen hohen Stellenwert. Mit seiner so engen Beziehung – in der Person Salomons – zu Haydn selbst und mit seiner Tauglichkeit als Aufführungsmaterial verbindet er Vorzüge miteinander, die sowohl für Wissenschaftler wie auch ausübende Musiker von Interesse sind. Wo Birchall von unseren übrigen Quellen abweicht (die Ursache besteht hauptsächlich in Änderungen, die Haydn nach seiner Rückkehr nach Wien vornahm und die Salomon deshalb unbekannt bleiben mußten), werden die Varianten neben anderen wesentlichen Lesarten in den Einzelanmerkungen unten ausgewiesen.

Editionsprinzipien

Überflüssige Vorsichts- oder wiederholte Akzidentien wurden in einigen Fällen gestrichen. Haydns Gewohnheit, in kontinuierlich modulierenden Passagen den Spielern solche Akzidentien zur Erinnerung fortwährend vorzuschreiben, selbst wenn sie dadurch im selben Takt wiederholt werden, erschwert es, dieses Prinzip konsequent durchzuhalten. In solchen Fällen wurden nur diejenigen Zeichen getilgt, die

Missing accidentals, staccato signs, slurs, ties and dynamics etc., have been added without comment only where their absence is the obvious result of the composer's, copyist's or engraver's oversight. Where explanatory comment may be helpful this will be found in the Textual Notes below.

Square brackets and broken ties and slurs indicate editorial additions in the text. The basis for such additions (i.e. parallel or analogous passages) will be clear by the context.

We have retained the indication *Tutti* (used by Haydn to cancel a previous *Solo*, usually in the woodwind) wherever it appears in our sources. Where it is clearly implied by the context but not shown in any of the sources, we have used the modern equivalent – [a 2] where the two parts are in unison.

Since Haydn and Elßler generally wrote a staccato as a quick stroke, it is difficult to determine whether a difference in performance is intended between a stroke and a dot. In general we have used dots except where a sharply accented staccato seems required.

SYMPHONY No. 103

The Symphony No. 103 was composed during Haydn's second visit to England (1794–95) and the autograph score has on its front page the date '$\overline{795}$' and 'Sinfonia in Es'. It was first performed under the composer's direction at the King's Theatre, Haymarket, London on 2 March 1795 at the fourth concert of G. B. Viotti's Opera Concert series and repeated at the seventh concert on 27 April. It will be recalled that Haydn's last three symphonies, although

nach heutigem Gebrauch den Spieler eher verwirren, als daß sie Klarheit schaffen.

Fehlende Akzidentien, Staccato-Zeichen, Artikulations- und Bindebögen, dynamische Bezeichnungen etc. wurden stillschweigend nur dann ergänzt, wenn sie offensichtlich vom Komponisten, Kopisten oder Stecher übersehen wurden. Wenn eine Erläuterung angebracht erscheint, ist sie unten in den Einzelanmerkungen zu finden.

Mit eckigen Klammern und als gestrichelte Bögen sind Herausgeberzusätze im Notentext gekennzeichnet. Die Begründung für solche Ergänzungen (parallele oder analoge Lesarten) ergibt sich aus dem Kontext.

Die Bezeichnung *Tutti*, die Haydn gewöhnlich in den Holzbläserstimmen verwendete, um ein voraufgegangenes *Solo* aufzuheben, wurde beibehalten, wo es in den benutzten Quellen erscheint. An Stellen, an denen eine Bezeichnung nach dem Kontext eindeutig erforderlich, in den Quellen jedoch nicht ersichtlich ist, wurde das heute übliche [a 2] gesetzt, wenn zwei Stimmen *unisono* spielen.

Da Haydn und Elßler die Staccato-Vorschrift in aller Regel als flüchtig dahingeworfenen Strich notierten, ist die Entscheidung schwierig, ob Strich und Punkt unterschiedlich ausgeführt werden sollen. Der Herausgeber hat grundsätzlich Punkte gesetzt, es sei denn, ein scharf akzentuiertes *staccato* schien gefordert.

SINFONIE Nr. 103

Haydn komponierte die Sinfonie Nr. 103 während seines zweiten England-Besuchs 1794/95. Auf dem Titelblatt der autographen Partitur stehen das Datum „$\overline{795}$" und „Sinfonia in Es". Die Erstaufführung fand unter der Leitung des Komponisten am 2. März 1795 beim fünften Konzert von Viottis „Opera Concerts" im Londoner King's Theatre am Haymarket statt; eine Wiederholung folgte im siebten Konzert am 27. April. Wie allseits bekannt, gab ur-

originally commissioned by Johann Peter Salomon for his own London concerts, were first given at Viotti's concerts, Salomon having discontinued his series at the beginning of 1795 because the war with France had made it impossible for him to obtain artists from the continent of 'the first talents'. Haydn's move to Viotti's series was made entirely with Salomon's blessing and the composer and his former impresario/concertmaster remained on the most cordial of terms; indeed, Salomon appeared frequently as soloist in the Opera Concert series.

Viotti's orchestra numbered some 60 players including, no doubt, doubled woodwind (and possibly brass) as evidenced by the 'solo' and 'tutti' indications in the orchestral parts. The *Andante* was encored at the first performance and the leader, William Cramer, singled out for special praise for his solo playing.

The autograph score was given by Haydn to Luigi Cherubini (1760–1842) in 1806 with the charming dedication over the composer's signature, 'Padre del celebre Cherubini/ ai 24tro de Febr. 806', when the latter visited him in Vienna. It was bought from Cherubini's grandson in 1879 by Julian Marshall from whom the British Museum acquired it not long thereafter.

An unsolved puzzle surrounds the Menuet, the first two pages of which in the autograph and the last page of the Trio are in a strange and somewhat unsteady hand. An annotation in the score by Julian Marshall suggests that the original pages were lost and were recopied by Cherubini, but H. C. Robbins Landon in his edition of the Symphony rejects that the handwriting is Cherubini's.[5] The paper is the same as the rest of the autograph in which there are a number of blank pages.

sprünglich Salomon Haydns letzte drei Sinfonien für seine eigenen Londoner Konzerte in Auftrag, doch wurden sie in Viottis Konzerten vorgestellt, nachdem Salomon seine Konzertreihe Anfang 1795 eingestellt hatte: Der Krieg mit Frankreich hatte es ihm unmöglich gemacht, vom europäischen Festland Künstler „allererster Güte" zu bekommen. Haydns Wechsel zu den Konzerten Viottis fand durchaus mit Salomons Billigung statt; der Komponist und sein vorheriger Impresario-Konzertmeister blieben auf überaus freundlichem Fuß. Salomon trat sogar häufig in den Opera Concerts als Solist auf.

Viottis Orchester zählte etwa 60 Spieler, darunter ohne Zweifel doppelt besetzte Holzbläser (und möglicherweise Blechbläser), wie aus den „solo"- und „tutti"-Eintragungen in den Orchesterstimmen hervorgeht. Das *Andante* wurde bei der Uraufführung wiederholt; der Konzertmeister, William Cramer, wurde wegen seines Solospiels besonders hervorgehoben.

Im Jahre 1806 überreichte Haydn die autographe Partitur an Luigi Cherubini (1760–1842), der ihn in Wien besuchte, mit einer reizenden Widmung über der Signierung des Komponisten: „Padre del celebre Cherubini/ai 24tro de Febr. 806". Julian Marshall erwarb es 1879 von Cherubinis Enkel, nicht lange darauf ging es in den Besitz des British Museum über.

Ein nicht gelöstes Rätsel gibt das Menuet auf, dessen erste zwei Seiten des Autographs und die letzte Seite des Trio von einer unbekannten und ein wenig unsicheren Hand stammen. Eine Anmerkung Julian Marshalls in der Partitur läßt vermuten, daß die Originalseiten verlorengegangen waren und von Cherubini noch einmal abgeschrieben wurden. H. C. Robbins Landon bestreitet in seiner Ausgabe der Sinfonie jedoch, daß es sich um Cherubinis Handschrift handele[5]. Das Papier ist dasselbe wie beim übrigen Autograph, worin einige Seiten unbeschrieben sind.

[5] *Joseph Haydn, the complete symphonies*, ed. H. C. Robbins Landon, Vol. XII, Vienna, 1968, p. LXXXI

[5] *Joseph Haydn, the complete symphonies*, hg. von H. C. Robbins Landon, Bd. XII, Wien, 1968, S. LXXXI

Sources

Autograph score in the British Library, London.........................AUT
Copy of the score made by London copyist, in the British Library, London........LON
Manuscript parts in the Esterházy Archives, Budapest, by Elßler and/or similar hand, some duplicate parts in another hand. There are two Vl. I parts, one marked 'Violino Primo Obl^to' with instrumental cues, but from which the first two pages (bb1–102) are missing. The Menuet is lacking in this source..........................BUD
Manuscript parts by Elßler, except for Vl. II and duplicate Vc/Cb. part which are in another hand, in the Fürstenberg Archives, Donaueschingen...................D/E
Printed parts by Birchall.............BIR
Birchall's edition of Salomon's Quintet arrangement......................SAL5

Harry Newstone

Quellen

Autographe Partitur in der British Library, London.........................AUT
Partiturabschrift eines Londoner Kopisten, British Library, London.............LON
Handschriftliche Stimmen im Esterházy Archiv, Budapest, in Elßlers oder einer ähnlichen Handschrift, einigere weitere Stimmendoppel von anderer Hand. In zwei Stimmen der Violine I, von denen eine „Violino Primo Obl^to" bezeichnet ist, sind Stichnoten eingetragen, doch fehlen bei beiden die ersten zwei Seiten (T. 1–102). Das Menuet fehlt in dieser Quelle ganz..........BUD
Handschriftliche Stimmen von Elßler, außer von Violine II und Doppeln der Stimme Vc./Kb. von anderer Hand, Fürstenberg-Archiv, Donaueschingen ....D/E
Gedruckte Stimmen von Birchall......BIR
Birchalls Ausgabe von Salomons Arrangement für Quintett.................SAL5

Harry Newstone

Textual Notes

Str. = Strings
Ww. = Woodwind
a/h = another hand
b(b) = bar(s)
n(n) = note(s)

Mov. I

bar 1 The famous drum roll from which the symphony gets its name is in AUT simply marked 'Solo' and 'Intrada' both here and when it returns at b201 – these indications followed in all our manuscript sources. LON also has 'Entrata' in a/h here but nothing at b201; BIR Timp. has only 'Solo' in both places. There is no dynamic indication in any of our sources except for D/E, which has $\Longleftarrow\Longrightarrow$ in a/h. D/E has many such additional markings, some in Haydn's hand but most in one or more hands of unknown provenance. Accordingly, any D/E (a/h) readings unsupported by another source but adopted in this edition are identified as such in textual notes. (The drum roll is of course not reproducible in SAL5, which has *fmo* $\Longleftarrow\Longrightarrow$ in Str., *ff tremolo* for Piano). Haydn's notation for a drumroll is 𝄍 , repeated semiquavers usually being written out.

6–7, Fg. slur from D/E (a/h), BIR; we add this to Vc., Cb. (Cb.
12–13 AUT, LON have slur bb12–13); bb12–13 Cor. 1/2 slur from LON (a/h?), BIR

13 Ob. 2 as D/E, LON, BIR; AUT, BUD g″ (as Ob. 1)

18–19 Vl. II, Vc/Cb. slurs from BIR

24–25 Ob. 1 slur as D/E (a/h), BIR, but other sources slur nn1–2 b24 only; Ob. 2 slur from LON, D/E, BIR; Vla. slur, Vc., Cb. slurs to b25, from LON, BIR

30–32 Ob. 1/2 phrasing from LON (a/h), b32 D/E (a/h), in which source also applied to Vl. II bb31–33 (so also possible for Vla.)

33–34 Vc., Cb. BIR slur across barline; b34 Fg. slur from D/E (a/h)

35–38 Vl. II D/E (a/h) phrased as Fg.

38 Fg., Str. *pp* from LON where second *p* added (by Haydn?), D/E (a/h) Vl. II, Vla., Vc/Cb., BIR; AUT, BUD *p*

40, 42,   Vl. I semiquaver slurs from LON, BIR; this slur AUT only
44, 46   b105, but all other sources bb104–106 (Vl. I), BIR Vc.,
Cb. bb105–108, also Vl. II b108

41–42,   Vla. AUT originally ♪|♪ changed to ♪|♪ apparently
161–162 after BUD, D/E were copied as they still have staccs.;
LON, BIR have the slur and also apply logically to next
two notes and across barline to b43 (also Vl. II here),
b163

46, 165   Vc., Cb. nn2–3 slur from BIR, ditto LON b165

47–49   Ob. AUT no phrasing; LON bb47, 49 nn3–5 slur, b48
nn2–5, these added in D/E in what may be Haydn's
hand; BIR these quavers stacc. (also bb166–168)

47–50   Fg. AUT 'col Contrabasso' from b48, LON at b47 'Col
Violoncelli'; BIR Vc. part for Fg.; error not repeated at
b166

51, 52   Vl. I (Fl.) nn5–10 slurs LON [musical notation] (ditto SAL5),
BUD [musical notation] AUT b50 (only) [musical notation] (slur even
shorter at b170), D/E (partly a/h), BIR [musical notation] and
b169, where BUD slurs Fl. [musical notation], Vl. I [musical notation]

53   LON Fg. [musical notation] Vc. [musical notation], these parts reversed
in BIR (SAL5 Vc. as LON); Vl. I LON, BIR b53 nn5–10,
b54 nn1–6 phrased [musical notation], ditto BIR bb172, 173
which phrasing we follow

53, 54   AUT *fz* only in Vla., Vc/Cb. (Fg.); LON, D/E, BUD *fz* also
to Vl. II, BIR *fz* all parts except Ob. 1, Timp.; LON (a/h)
sf in Fl., Timp. (the latter possibly applicable also to
Cor., Tr.); LON, BIR Fl. slurs b53 nn3–4, b54 nn4–5; BIR
slurs Fl. b54 nn1–2, Cl. b53 nn4–5, b54 nn1–2

54   Timp. LON n5 changed (a/h) to e♭, so printed in BIR (if
adopted could possibly apply to n4 bb55, 56)

57, 58   AUT *fz* only in Vl. I/II, Vla., added in LON (a/h) to Ob.,
Cl., Tr., Timp., so printed in BIR where also added to
Fg., Vc/Cb.; LON Vl. I, D/E (a/h) Ob. 1, Cl. 1, Vl. II, BIR
Vl. I/II (SAL5 Vl. I/II) phrased [musical notation] ; b57
Fg., Vc/Cb. semiquaver slurs from LON, D/E (a/h), BIR,
fz from BIR. These comments apply in general to bb109,
110 where D/E (a/h) Ob. 1, BIR Ob. 2 are phrased
[musical notation] which we adopt and apply to Fl., Cl. 1/2.

58 Ob. 1/2 *p* from D/E (a/h) Ob. 1, also b61, where printed in BIR

59 Cl. 2 D/E (a/h) $4\frac{1}{2}$ bars rest, BUD, BIR 5 bars rest; LON 'unis' at b60 (i.e., as Cl. 1 until middle of b64)

60 Cl., Fg., Str. D/E (a/h) semiquavers slur (Fg., Vl. I, Vl. II? slur reaches b61 n1); ditto b62 Fg., Str. (Vl. I, Vc/Cb. slur reaches b63 n1)

62 Str. (under b♭/B♭) LON *fz*, AUT *fz* Vla. only

63, 64 Fl., Ob., Cl., Vl. I/II *fz* (*sf*) from LON (a/h, Salomon's?), BIR; Vl. I/II AUT b63 n4 *f* copied in LON as *fz* then crossed out and *sf* added in a/h to last note

65, 66 Ob., Cl., b66 Cor. *fz* from LON, BIR, partly D/E; Vl. II BIR *sf* in parallel with Vl. I, Vla. (also SAL5); Cor. 1/2 tie from BIR

65–67 Ob., Cl. slurs from BIR; ditto D/E (a/h) Ob. 1, Cl. 1, Vla.

67, 69 Vc/Cb. n4 *fz* from BIR (LON b69); b67 Fg., Vl. I LON n1 *fz* (SAL5 all parts), BIR Vl. I n1 *f*

69 Vl. I BIR n2 slurred to n1 b70, where AUT has *fz*, LON *fz* and *ff*, all other sources *ff*

72–73 Ob. 2 slur from BIR, likely for Ob. 1, Fg.; D/E (a/h) Ob. 1 b72 n2 to b73 n1 slur, Cl. 1 slur over bb71–72 (possibly intended to reach b73), Fg. b71 nn1–2 slur; Cor., Tr. tie from LON (a/h), BIR

73, 74 Fg., Vla., Vc/Cb. stacc. from BIR which also has slur b74 n4 to b75 n1; ditto bb213–215 Vla., Vc/Cb. but this time slur (to b215) only in Vc/Cb.

78 Fg. n2 as LON (col Vc.), D/E, BIR (also on basis of b178); AUT, BUD second half of bar rest

79 Ob. 1 *p* from D/E (a/h); b180 similar *p* from BIR

79, 80, (and bb143, 144, 147, 148, 179, 180, 183, 184) Ob. 1,
83, 84, Vl. I, bb144, 148 Fl., slurs partly in LON, D/E (a/h), consistently in BIR though the 3-quaver slurs sometimes ♩ ♫ , sometimes ♩ ♫

82 Vl. II slur from AUT but nothing at bb146, 182 where Vl. II, Vla. slurs are in LON, D/E (both a/h), BIR; Vla. slur from LON (a/h), BIR

87–90 Fg., Vla., Vc/Cb. stacc. from BIR

94 Vl. II slur to b95 from BIR, D/E (a/h), ditto Vl. I
bb95–96 BIR only

95 Fg. 'Solo' in D/E (a/h), in BUD passage written for both
parts; BIR beat 2 dotted crotchet d′

97 Vla. slur on basis of Fg. (D/E, a/h, has slur over
bb96–97 both parts); LON |♩ ♪ 𝄽 𝄽| followed by 5½
bars rest (SAL5 e♮′ rises to f′, then 5 bars rest)

98 Vl. I, Vla. slur possible on basis of Vc. slur (all sources)

105, 106 D/E (a/h) Fl. phrasing
Ob. 1 |♩ ♪♬♩|♩ ♪♬♩| , the same semi-
quaver slurs in Vl. II bb107, 108; we adopt this and
show as possible for Vl. II, Vla. bb105, 106 where
there is no phrasing any source. Fl. b105 *cresc.* from
LON, BIR, Ob. *cresc.* from BIR where it appears at end of
b105

109 Fg., Vc/Cb. slurs from BIR; Vl. I BIR slur from b108 to
n1; Vla. *fz* from D/E (a/h)

109–110 Ob. 1 phrasing from D/E (a/h), Ob. 2 phrasing from BIR,
added to Fl., Cl. by analogy; Vl. I/II phrasing from
LON, BIR (D/E nothing, b109 Vl. I BUD nn1–6 stacc.)

111–113 Cb. AUT
(i.e., notes *and* rests), next 6 bars empty (Cb. continues
as Vc.?), then bb120–122 (in small notes)

at b125 etc. This Cb. passage
(bb111–124) is in none of the sources and suggests that
it was either an afterthought and that Haydn forgot to
erase the rests in bb111–113, or that he decided to omit
the Cb. from this passage and forgot to erase the notes.

122 Vla. AUT originally or ,
the latter reading in LON, (SAL5)

124 Fl. 1 D/E (a/h) —— (logical in view of Str. *cresc.*)
suggested for Ob. 1/2; Ob. 1/2, Vla. beat 2 slur from
LON, also BIR which slurs Ob. 2 likewise and slurs Fl. to
b125

125, 126 Vl. I/II phrasing from BIR; D/E (a/h) this too in Vl. II
but ♩♩♩♩♩♩ in Vl. I; b126 Vl. II n11 f″ from AUT,
other sources c″ (as Vl. I)

126, 127   Ob. 1/2 LON, BIR ,

        Ob. 1 e♮″ (b126), Ob. 2 (b127) being alterations in LON (a/h?)

133   Vl. I LON, BUD, Vl. II LON nn5, 6 stacc.; BIR Fg. nn2–6 stacc. but D/E n6 slur to b134; Vl. I n6 slur to b134 from D/E, BIR

136   Vc. BIR nn1–2 no slur, n2 to b137 slur

139   Cl. 2 written into LON (a/h, Haydn's), printed in BIR

142   Fl. c″ written into LON, D/E (both a/h), printed in BIR but missing in AUT, BUD, (SAL5)

143   Fg. slur to b144 faint in AUT, clear in D/E and bb147–148

149   Fl. D/E (a/h) changed from ♩. to ♩. ♩. (possible)

150   Vl. I n6 ♮ only in BIR

152–154   Cl., Fg. slurs from D/E (a/h) where Ob. 1 has ♩. | ♩. ♩.| ♩. ♩. | ; Fg. AUT slur (b152) probably meant to continue after page turn, this slur in LON but crossed out; LON, BIR tie bb152–153 in Ob. only

153   Cor. f from Cor. 1 BUD; Tr., Timp. f by analogy; AUT, LON, BIR no dynamic for these, D/E (a/h) Cor. 1/2 p (!), Tr. 2 ff

156–157   Fg., Str. semiquaver slurs inconsistent in sources – AUT, LON, BUD slur only last group Vl. II b157, BIR slurs both groups; D/E (a/h), SAL5 more general semiquaver slurs, D/E even b155 Vl. II first group (all 5 notes)

156–158   Cl. 1/2 slur from LON (a/h), BIR (where Cl. 2 slur reaches only to b157); bb156–157 Cor. 1/2, Tr. 1/2, tie from LON, BIR, Cor. only D/E (a/h); b158 Cl. stacc. from AUT, LON, BIR, could apply generally or at least to Ob.

159ff.   AUT, excepting Vl. II n1, has only the Vl. I part with the instruction (Haydn's) 'Come Sopra', adding the amended Vla., Vc/Cb. parts at b175 and resuming full scoring at b176; NB, b167 Vl. I n2 Haydn this time writes b♭′ instead of quaver rest as at b48; BUD has the quaver rest in b167

178   Vla. n2 a♭ as AUT, LON, D/E, changed D/E (a/h) to b♭; BUD, BIR b♭, (SAL5 a♭)

179–185 Cor. 'Soli', slurs from LON (a/h), BIR; bb181–182 slur from BIR; b185 LON, BIR slur reaches n1 b186

186 Cor., Tr., Timp. *f* from BIR

187 Vla. nn4–6 g as AUT, BUD, SAL5; LON (a/h) changed to b♭, D/E, BIR b♭

188, 190, Timp. ═══ from D/E (a/h); Ww. BIR *ff*; bb190, 192
192 Cor., Tr. *ff* from BUD, BIR

189–190 Tr. AUT tie (Cor. 'Col Clarini'); D/E Cor. ties but scratched out in Tr.; BUD, BIR no ties, which we follow; LON Cor., Tr. no ties bb188–193

193 Vl. I AUT ═══ missing, ditto D/E and *fz*

194 General *f* as BIR (except Tr., Vl. I, Timp.); AUT no general dynamic (preceding *ff* may still apply), LON *f* in some parts, ditto D/E (a/h) Fl., Fg., Cor. 1 (*fz*), Timp., Vl. II, Vla. (*fz*)

197 Vl. I *p* as it appears in AUT; BUD *p* n4, originally so LON before being crossed out and replaced (a/h) under n1, where found in BIR; D/E (a/h) ═══ , b198 *p*; SAL5 no *p* until b199

199–200 Vl. I slur from LON, BIR, SAL5

206–207 Fl., Ob., Cl. slur from D/E (a/h), BIR; Cor. 1 tie from LON (a/h?), BIR, Cor. 2 slur from BIR; Vc/Cb. slur from LON (a/h?)

212–213 Ww., Cor. slurs from BIR, partly D/E (a/h); Vl. I slur all sources but LON, SAL5

217–218 Ob. 2, Cl. 2, Cor. 2 BIR tie

219 Cor. phrasing, 'Soli' from BUD, D/E (a/h), BIR; LON (a/h) has quaver slurs, no dots or 'Soli'

220 Ob., Fg. phrasing from LON (a/h), D/E (a/h), BIR; Ob. 'Soli' from BUD (suggested for Fg.)

221 Vla., Vc/Cb. stacc. by analogy with Vl. I/II from LON, BIR; D/E (a/h) continues phrasing Ww. ♩ ♪♩ ♪|♩. , Tr., Vl. I/II, Vla. ♫♫♫♫♩|♪ ; Fg. 2 BIR n3 g

222–225 Fg., Vla., Vc/Cb. stacc. from BIR

227 Vl. I n1 quaver all sources

Mov. II

AUT: *più tosto Allegretto* was later added under *Andante* and signed by Haydn, presumably after our manuscript sources were copied as the amendment is in none of them, or BIR or SAL5

1, 5 (and 51, 55, 59, 63) Vl. I/II slur ♩ ♫ all sources fairly consistently; AUT Vl. I (II) slur does not quite reach n3 but looks as though it was intended to most times

3, 53, 61 Vl. I/II consensus favours ♩♫♩ ; b3 LON, BIR nn1–4 slur, b61 BIR n4 stacc.

16 Vl. I BIR nn2–4 slur, D/E (a/h), BIR nn6–8 (also Vl. II) slur (AUT, LON no phrasing)

17 Vla., Vc/Cb. n3 stacc. all sources (except D/E Vla. slur nn1–3 in a/h), b19 nn1–3 slur all sources except BUD (nn1–2 slur), BIR (n3 stacc.)

23, 81 Vl. I nn1–4 phrasing as AUT, LON; b23 D/E (a/h)

♩♫♩♫♩ , BIR ♩♫♩♫♩ , b81 D/E

♫♫♫ , BIR ♫♫♫

26 Ob. (also Cor. b27, Fg. b29) *p* from LON (in Haydn's hand), BIR; Vl. I n1 stacc. from LON, D/E, BIR (added to Vl. II and at b84)

27, 28 Vl. I/II AUT phrased | ♩♫♫ | ♩♫♫ | (ditto Ob. 1/2 but stacc. only n4 b28); b27 LON Vla. *fz* crossed out, BIR Vla., Vc/Cb. *p*, also Vc/Cb. b43,. Fg. b45

30 Vla. LON, BIR, SAL5 n1 *fz*, not b46 where BUD, D/E (a/h) have it

31 Vla. *fz* by analogy with b27

35–37 Vc/Cb. LON, BIR, SAL5 n1 *fz*, also b38 LON Vla., BIR Vc/Cb.

36, 38 Vl. II *fz* all sources but AUT, BUD; n2 d♯ (and bb144, 146 plus Ob. 2)? (See also bb143, 145 below.)

39 Dynamics as AUT; LON Vc/Cb. *p*; BIR Ob. *pp*, b38 n3 Vla., Vc/Cb. *pp*; D/E (a/h) Vla. b38 n3 *pp*, b39 *ppp*

41 Vc/Cb. slur from BIR, possible for Vl. II, Vla.

53 Ob. 1 *p* from D/E (a/h), BIR

55 Ob. 1 D/E (a/h) slur extended to b56 n1 (as AUT bb63–64 Fl., Ob.); in both places BUD, LON, BIR slur only within bb55, 63

57, 65 Ob. 1 phrasing from D/E (a/h), BIR; ditto b65 Fl., Ob. LON, Fl. BIR

66–67 Vl. I AUT, LON phrased ♪│♩ ♫ ; BUD, D/E, BIR slur across barline to n1 b67

74 Fg. 'Solo' from D/E (in Haydn's hand); Vl. I LON, D/E (a/h), BIR (also Vl. II nn2–4) ♩. ♫ ♫. ♩ ♫. ♩ , BUD ♩. ♫ ♩. ♫ ♩ ; Vl. II D/E (not Elßler) n1 changed to crotchet

75 Fg. AUT nn2–3 slur but Vla. n3 stacc. (as b17)

83, 84 Fl., Ob. phrasing only in BIR, also b84 Fl. stacc. which we apply to Ob.

84/85 Vl. Solo, Rip., b85 Vl. II, Vla., Vc/Cb. *p* from BIR; b85 LON Vc/Cb. *p* in Haydn's hand

85 Vl. Rip. AUT slur almost reaches n4, is shorter at b89, clearly nn1–4 at b101; BUD, D/E, BIR slur nn1–3 bb85, 89, nn1–4 b101, each time BIR n4 stacc.; LON slur nn1–2 b101; BIR Vl. Solo slur nn2–4 b85, possibly intended nn1–4 as b101 where n4 has stacc.

86 Vl. Solo LON, D/E (both a/h) nn8–10 stacc. dots under triplet slur; SAL5 these notes stacc.

88 Vl. Rip. BIR n2 g

89–91, Vl. Solo phrasing (and grace note, written ♪) from BUD; D/E (a/h) phrasing b89 nn7–12 ♫♪ ♫♪ , b90 nn1–2, b91 nn7–8, bb104, 107 nn1–2 slurs

93–94, Fg. slurs from BIR, also D/E (a/h) Fg. 1 which has slur
95–96 bb94–95; Cor. slurs by analogy; Cor *p* from LON (a/h), BIR

108 Vla. LON, BUD, BIR nn1–3, 4–6 slur (possibly triplet sign rather than phrasing); D/E nn1–3 faint slur, also dots on all notes and 'Solo' (both a/h)

109 Vl. I AUT see b1 Textual Note which applies also here (sources again have mixture of ♩ ♫ , ♩ ♫ sometimes with stacc. n4)

112 Vl. I AUT may originally have read [musical notation] (the slur is still visible)

113 Vl. I slur by analogy (see b5 Textual Note)

116 Fg. BIR as Vc.; Vc. LON phrased ♩. ♫ ♩ ♪

117 Str. LON, BIR Vl. I, Vc/Cb. *ff*; bb117, 118 D/E (a/h), (SAL5) nn1–8 slur

119–121 Vl. II, Vla. phrasing from D/E, BIR, added to Vc/Cb. b119

122, 123 Vl. I slurs from D/E (a/h), BIR

124 Vl. I nn10–11 slur from BIR (and b131); AUT Cor. 2 not written but 'coi Clarini', D/E, BIR Cor. 2 as Cor. 1; LON, BUD Cor. 2 as Tr. 2

125 Fg. D/E, BIR whole-bar slurs, ditto Vla. D/E (a/h); Vl. I slurs from LON, BIR, (SAL5), ditto b127 (not LON); bb125, 127 D/E (a/h) nn1–8, 9–16 slur

132 Vl. I/II stacc. from LON, BIR, (SAL5)

133 Ob. 1 slur from LON (a/h), BIR (slur possible Ob. 2, performed 𝅘𝅥𝅮); Vl. I/II BIR nn1–8 slurred in pairs; D/E (a/h), (SAL5) nn1–8 slur (possibly two 4-note slurs supported by faint slur over second group in AUT); Cor. 1, Tr. 1 LON, BUD, BIR n1 c″, D/E Cor. 1 d″, Tr. 1 c″

134 Ob. n3 *p* from BIR, 'Soli' from D/E (a/h); Cor. 1/2, Tr. 1/2 slurs from LON, BIR

135 Cor. *p* from LON (Haydn's hand), BIR; Vl. II, Vla. *p* from D/E (a/h), applied to Vl. I, Vc/Cb., also Fg.

136 Fl. 'Solo', *p* from D/E (a/h), BIR; phrasing (also bb138, 140) from D/E (a/h); b141 phrasing from SAL5

143, 145 Ob. 2, Fg., Vla. n2 ♯ from LON, D/E (both a/h), BIR; the cautionary ♮ in bb144, 146 (Ob. 2 n4, Vla. nn1, 2) from BIR

144, 145, Vl. II *fz* from BIR; also possible for Vla. bb143, 145
146

147 Fl., Vl. I phrasing from LON, D/E (both a/h), BIR; Ob. 1 slur from LON (a/h), BIR; Fg., Vla. slur from D/E (a/h) where LON (a/h), BIR have stacc. quavers; b148 Fg., Vla. slur from D/E (a/h), ditto LON Fg. which also has two 2-note slurs added in (a/h) as do Ob. 1, 2, Vl. II, Vla., ditto BIR except Vl. II

149 Ob. 1 slur from D/E (a/h), ditto Fg., Vla. slur reaching b150

153, 189 Tr. 1/2 LON nn1–2 slur, ditto BIR but b189 slurs continue to b190

154 Fl., Vl. I/II, Vla. *fz* from BIR, D/E (a/h); *fz* AUT, BUD only in Ob., Vc/Cb., LON only in Ob., Vl. I

157, 159, Staccs. mostly from BIR
193, 195

160 Tr. 2 LON, BIR e (as b158 but quaver)

162 Vl. I BIR nn1–4 slur; Vla. AUT originally *p* changed to *fz*
(an example of Haydn's use of this mark for a phrase
rather than a single note); LON *for* (smudged/erased?);
BUD, D/E *fz* but crossed through in D/E (a/h) and *p* written in three times (!) above and below the stave; BIR,
(SAL5) no *fz*

163–164 Vc. tie from LON (a/h), BIR, (SAL5)

174 Cor., Tr. *f* from AUT, D/E, BIR; LON, BUD *ff*; Vl. I nn2–3

slur from D/E (a/h?); LON, BIR

175, 176 Vl. II lower note as LON where g is changed to b♭ (as
b174), so written in D/E (not Elßler, b175 only), printed
in BIR

179 Fl. from LON where originally for Ob. 1, crossed out
and written into Fl. in Haydn's hand (clearly authentic),

so printed in BIR; b180 Fl. originally

182–183, Fl. slurs from BIR
184–185

194 Fl. 2 BIR n1 quaver

196 Str. LON *ff*, bb196–198 Vc. as Cb.

Mov. III

AUT: The first 21 bars (two pages) of the Menuet and
the last 8 bars (one page) of the Trio are in an unknown, rather unsteady, hand; the present edition refers
to these as 'AUT'. The whole Menuet is missing in BUD.

1 General *f* from BIR; Vl. I (-1) alone has *f* in 'AUT'; Cl. 1
D/E (a/h) has 'tacet' top of page which may have some
bearing on why some modern editions lack clarinets in
this movement, but the reference is to Mov. II

5, 36 All parts (but Timp.) LON (a/h), BIR minim to crotchet
slur, also D/E (a/h) most wind parts, Vla.

6–7 Ob. 2, Fg., Cor. 2, Vl. II, Vla., Vc/Cb. D/E (a/h) slur
across barline, also BIR (not Cor.); ditto bb37–38 plus
D/E (a/h) Ob. 1, but not Cor. either source

11 Vl. I upbeat *legato* from BIR; LON no *legato*

15–16 Vl. II, Vc/Cb. slur by analogy with Vla. (Vla. as D/E, BIR); Cl. 1, Fg., Cor. 1 slur (also bb17–18) from LON (a/h), D/E (a/h), BIR

16 Vl. I LON, BIR, (SAL5) nn1–3 slur

20–21, Cl. slurs from BIR; bb22–23 Ob. 2 tie from BIR; bb20–22

22–23 Fg. D/E (a/h) long slur possibly meant to reach b24

22 AUT resumes in Haydn's hand

24, 26 Cl., Cor., Tr. slur to bb25, 27 from BIR, bb26–27 Cor. 1 slur in LON (a/h)

35 Fg. n3 all sources ♩ , editorially adjusted to ♪⁷ on basis of Fl., Vl. I; Vl. I *fz* in BIR only

37 Cor. 2 BIR has Tr. 2 part in error; Cor. LON originally omitted but first bar of entry written in a/h with 'etc.' sign in b38

37–40 Tr., bb38–40 Cor. stacc. from LON, BIR, ditto bb46–48 where Ob., Cl. stacc. in BIR

39, 41, Quaver slurs from LON (a/h), BIR, D/E (Fl. only, a/h)
43

42 AUT Tr. originally [musical notation], Timp. [musical notation], both crossed out

44 Ob., Cl., Fg., Cor., Tr. AUT no tie to b45 (page turn after b44) but other sources mostly show continuous chord bb43–46 (D/E Fg. to b47), except LON, D/E Cl. bb44–45 no tie

46 Ob. 1 D/E (a/h) n1–b47 n1 slur; Fg. tie to b47 from D/E (a/h); Tr. 1 D/E (a/h) nn1–2 slur

Trio Quaver phrasings generally from D/E (partly a/h) which standardizes [musical notation] pattern where AUT Str. unclear, Cl., Fg. non-existent, and where LON, BIR have [musical notation] (b51 Vl. II) or [musical notation] (b52 Vla. where LON has [musical notation]); b53 Vc. AUT nn5–6 originally slur, curiously changed to stacc., so copied LON and at first D/E but there the slur reinstated (a/h) under the stacc.; BIR has slur; same observations apply b77 where 'AUT' (not Haydn's hand) has [musical notation]

55 Fg. 2 BIR note f (as b79)

65 Vl. II AUT n1 originally minim (probably [musical notation]); D/E (a/h), BIR, (SAL5) nn1–3 slur

69   Vl. II slur from LON, BIR

72   'AUT' again unknown hand to end of Trio; upbeat to bb73ff. quaver phrasings from D/E (a/h)

79   Vc. 'AUT' beat 3 rest (as b55), B♭ only on Cb. stave

Mov. IV

1   Cor. no dynamic any source except D/E (a/h) *p*; BIR *p* b5 (implying *f* b1); SAL5 *f* b1, *p* b5; NB, LON *p* b45 in Haydn's hand

9   Cl. *p* from LON (a/h), BIR; bb10, 11 Cl. 2 phrasing from BIR, also D/E (a/h) which lacks b10 slur but has Cl. 1 b11 slur; comments apply also at bb49–51, 162–164

25–27   Ob. 1 slurs from BIR, also bb25, 26 D/E (a/h), b26 LON; b27 Vl. I slur from LON (a/h), BIR

39ff.   Vl. II, Vla. slurs follow BUD extending Vla. to b45 as Vl. II; AUT slurs unclear; bb44–45 Fg. slur from LON

62   Vla. n1 as AUT, LON, D/E, (SAL5); BUD b♭, BIR f, both changes possibly to avoid parallel octaves with Vl. I

63   Vl. I slurs on basis of b62 (where D/E, a/h, has whole-bar slur); Vla. slur from D/E (a/h), ditto Vl. I slurs b64 (cf. b72)

76   Cor. 1 D/E, BIR c″

77   Ob. 2, Cl. 1/2 slurs from LON (a/h), BIR (Cl. only); Fl., Vl. I by analogy

78, 80   Fg., Vc/Cb. quaver slur from BIR, ditto Fl. b83, Vl. I by analogy; (b78 Vl. I SAL5 nn1–4 slur)

85–86   Fg. BIR no tie (ditto bb87–88), presumably to facilitate *fz*

86, 88   Fl., Vl. I slur as D/E, BIR; AUT, BUD, (SAL5) Vl. I (Fl.) slur reaches only to n2; Ob., Cl. slur across barline from D/E (a/h), BIR

90   Fg. 2 n3 f from AUT, D/E; LON n3 a (as Vla. n4) with ♮ added (a/h); BUD, BIR a (no ♮ BUD); Vla. nn2–4 (Fg. nn1–3) slur (not Vl. I)

92   Vl. I n2 AUT originally minim; Fl. all sources n2 minim (except SAL5 crotchet)

95   LON copyist here wrote b97 in Cl. and at b97 wrote b99 in Cor., Tr., thus getting two bars out until b107 (further evidence that this score was compiled from a set of parts), corrected in a/h

103–104 Fl. slur added on basis of bb101–102 and D/E (a/h)

104, 105 Fl. slurs from D/E (a/h); bb104–105 Cl. 2 BIR tie

107 Cor., Tr., Timp., Vc/Cb. crotchet as LON, BIR and all sources b316; AUT, BUD, D/E minim (D/E Cor. 2 changed to crotchet in a/h)

128, 130 Fg. D/E (a/h) minims slurred, also bb131–133 slur; ditto bb236, 238, 239–240, these D/E (a/h) slurs also in bb242, 244, 245–246 (Ob. 1), 331 (Cl. 1, Fg.), 333, 334–335 (Fl., Fg.), 337 (Fg.), 339 (Fl., Fg.), 340–341 (Cl. 1, Fg.)

133 LON writes bar once with repeat sign and 'bis' over it, thus Fg. has 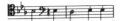 ; bb133–134 BIR

135–138 Ww. stacc. from BIR; ditto bb342–345 Ob. 1, Fg., Vla., Vc/Cb.

178–179 Vl. I slur as BUD, Vl. II all sources, Ob. 1 D/E (a/h); AUT slur barely reaches into b179

185 Fg. n1 BUD has crotchet rest

189 Fl., Ob. stacc. from BIR; Vl. I/II stacc. from LON, BIR, (SAL5); Vla. nn1–3 stacc. in AUT, added to n4, Fg. nn1–4

190 Fg. 2 BIR *ff*; Timp. *ff* from BIR

205–206 Vla. slur on basis of Vl. I (where AUT originally was something like ⟨score⟩); Vla. D/E (a/h) long slur bb204–206; Vl. I BUD no tie across barline

211 Ww., Str. n2 *fz* as BIR, LON (except Cl.); AUT, BUD, D/E *fz* in Vl. II only

214 Cl. 1 AUT, BUD, D/E n4 (a) has ♭, so in LON but corrected (a/h) to ♮; BIR f♮″; D/E (a/h) has ♮ beginning of next bar

216–217 Timp. AUT originally ⟨score⟩ ; so in LON but corrected in a/h

226–227 Fg. slur from D/E (a/h); Cl. bb230–231 by analogy
230–231

255 Fg. LON, D/E, BIR tenor clef middle of bar making n1 an impossible f, which is changed in LON (a/h) to a♭; BIR has a♭; in AUT the tenor clef appears to have been moved from the middle to the beginning of the bar, where it is in BUD; Tr. 2 AUT as Tr. 1 (after page turn), so in BUD, D/E; Tr. 2 LON (a/h), BIR c′ and ties from b254 for Cor., Tr.

259 Timp. LON note crossed out, BIR bar rest (obviously to avoid harmonic clash); Vla. D/E, Vc/Cb. all sources n1 stacc.

274 Vla. nn2–3 slur from D/E, BIR; Vc/Cb. nn2–3 slur from BIR, added to Fg.

275–276 Cor. slur from LON (a/h), BIR, D/E (a/h Cor. 2 only)

293 Cl. 1/2 n1 BIR, Cl. 2 BUD *fz*

304 Fg. adjusted to ♩ on basis of bb300, 302, 206; all sources ♩ ♪

311–312 Ob. 2, Cl. 1 BIR tie; bb313–314 Ob. 2, Cor. 2, Tr. 2 tie

313 Fl., Ob. 1 slur from LON (a/h, Haydn's?), D/E (a/h) Fl.; added to Cl. by analogy

321–322, Cor. slurs from LON (a/h), BIR, also D/E (a/h) Cor. 2
325–326

329 Fl. 'Solo', slur to b330 (also Fg.) from D/E (a/h)

330–341 Cl. 2 LON, BUD, BIR as Cl.; Cl. 1 still Solo from b323 in all sources

338–341 AUT originally as shown in Appendix 1, the new version of these 4 bars on a sheet at the end of the AUT score together with the new version of bb364–367 (see next entry), both, according to Landon, 'in Salomon's handwriting' (*Joseph Haydn, the complete symphonies*, ibid., p. LXXXII)

364–367 AUT originally 17 bars here as shown in Appendix 2 but crossed out and replaced by the new 4-bar version; at b363 AUT, BUD, D/E Ob. 1 n4 has g″ (left over from discarded version) which now should be c‴ as corrected in LON, BIR

364–366 Ob. 2, Cl. 1/2 bb364–365 tie from LON, BIR; Ob. 1 bb364–366, Fg., Cor. 1 bb365–366 D/E (a/h) slur; Cor. 2, Tr. 2 bb365–366 tie from BIR

368–371, Ob. 1/2, Fg., Tr. 1/2 D/E (a/h) 4-bar slur
372–375

376–377 Fl. LON, BIR nn1–2 slur, also D/E (a/h) Fl., Ob. 1/2, Fg., Tr. 1/2

Harry Newstone

SYMPHONY No. 103

In Nomine Domini

Joseph Haydn
(1732–1809)

I. Adagio

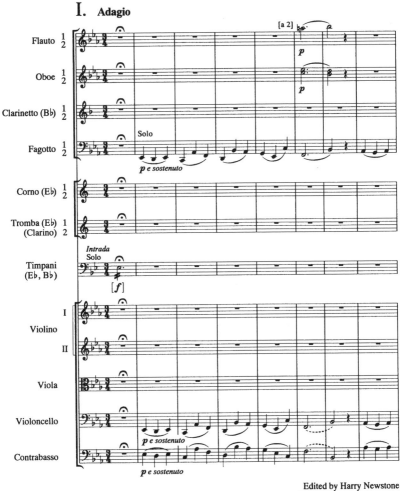

Edited by Harry Newstone
© 1996 Ernst Eulenburg Ltd
and Ernst Eulenburg & Co GmbH

4

Allegro con spirito

12

EE 7000

14

EE 7000

16

EE 7000

18

20

EE 7000

164
[a 2]
a 2
a 2
a 2
Fl. 1 2
Ob. 1 2
Cl. (B♭) 1 2
Fg. 1 2
Cor. (E♭) 1 2
Tr. (E♭) 1 2
Timp.
I
Vl.
II
Vla.
Vc.
Cb.
f

30

EE 7000

33

Finis Laus Deo

EE 7000

34

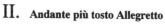

II. Andante più tosto Allegretto

EE 7000

45

EE 7000

46

EE 7000

48

EE 7000

EE 7000

50

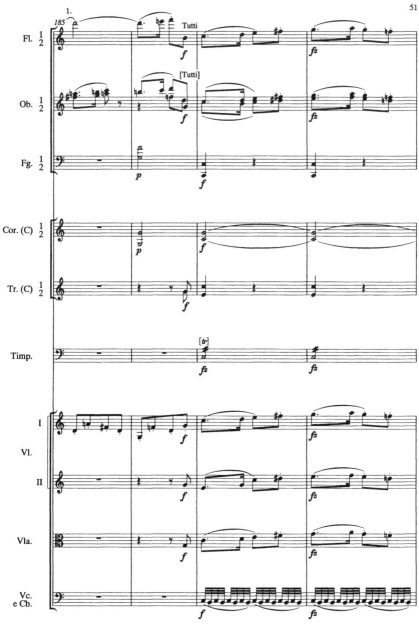

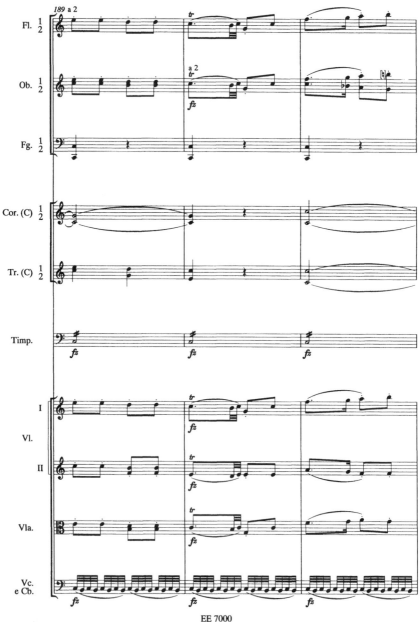

III. Menuet

57

EE 7000

58

EE 7000

60

Trio

EE 7000

61

EE 7000

62

Menuet da capo

IV. Finale

EE 7000

suspensions

imitations
continue

imitation reinforced in brass
staying on same note = F
continue

antiphonal contest
between horns + trumpets

EE 7000

70

EE 7000

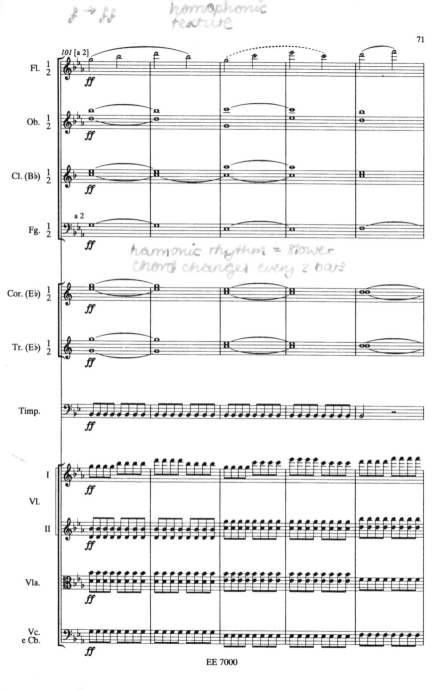

2nd
Subject → B♭ maj

cadential figure

EE 7000

extended
chromatically

dominant
7th
in E♭m

77

EE 7000

Key: Bb minor

82

melodic sequences

Fmaj chord

2nd beat of bar- disrupt rhythm

A dim⁷ chord

Coincides with change of

EE 7000

... returns to Eb = RECAPITULATION

90

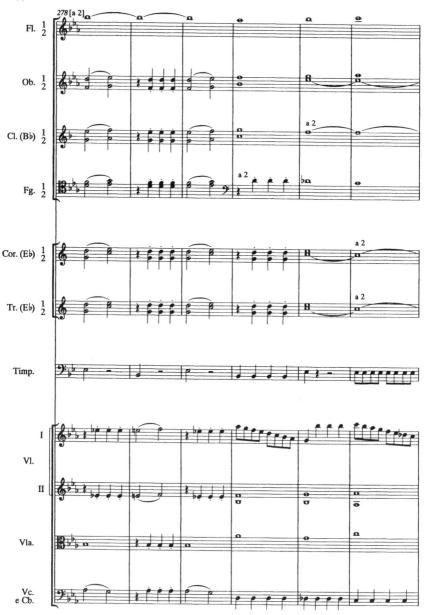

full orchestra enters
more quickly than
in exposition

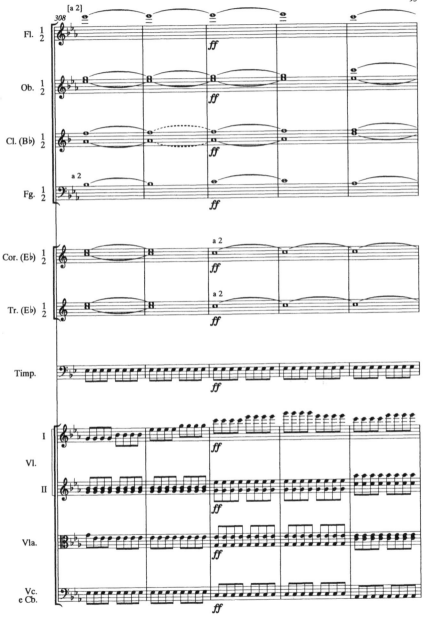

SECOND SUBJECT

E♭ minor

98

cadence figure

101

EE 7000

Fine Laus Deo

Appendix 1

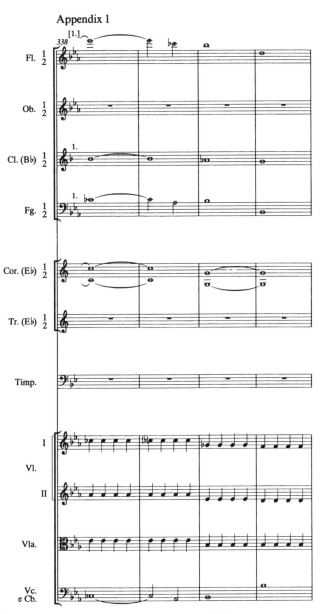

106

Appendix 2